Rock Paper Sc

A Life Guide to Living
Victoriously Over Abuse

Kristal Clark & Carla Yarborough

Life Chronicles Publishing
Give your life a voice!

http://www.mylifechronicles.org

ISBN-0692849467
ISBN-9780692849460

Editors:
Debrena Jackson-Gandy
Sahasha Campbell-Garbutt

Cover Design:
Adrian Sims
Life Chronicles Publishing Copyright © 2017

Rock: No matter what you throw at me.

Paper: No matter how you try to crumble me.

Scissors: No matter how you attempt to cut me down.

I AM AN OVERCOMER!!

Acknowledgements

Kristal's Acknowledgements:

I would like to first and foremost honor my husband, Derek Clark. You've shown me quitting is never an option.

To my beautiful daughters, Kenadi, Kacia, and Kiara you fill me with so much joy, hope, and unconditional love. My life would not be the same without you, three girls.

Vernon Brazzle, my father, you have set the standard high in my life, and I will never forget your fatherly love.

Annie Brazzle, my mother, you made sure that I did not go without one thing! For that, I am truly grateful.

My amazingly talented little sister, April Allen; you make me so proud. You are a powerhouse of talent.

To Karly Roshelle Doble, thank you for walking with me throughout my healing journey. You taught me how to trust and to be.

To my spiritual mother, Kim Jones-Pothier thank you for taking a risk on the vision placed in my heart. I love you! You are an answer to my prayers.

Carla's Acknowledgements:

Without the guidance of Sharon Blake of Life Chronicle's publishing company and her team, this book would have just been a dormant vision.

To the survivors who have courageously given us your voice to use, I thank each and every one of you.

I would also like to express my deepest gratitude to my grandmother, Irmagene Reed, who taught me strength in its greatest form.

I am beyond grateful for my mother, Monica Reed Harrison, who taught me unconditional love and showed me how to live in constant forgiveness.

I would also like to thank my warrior sister, Jean Wilson, who has shown me how to rise above adversity.

Finally, I would like to thank my soul sisters, Katina Lucero and Charlotte Reese who have given me decades of genuine friendships. I am because of you.

Contents

Acknowledgements..1

Foreword 5

Introduction 9

Chapter 1: Silence Killers 15

Chapter 2: Unmuted 21

Chapter 3: Overcomers 27

Chapter 4: Outliving Your Pain 33

Chapter 5: Redeemed from Regret 41

Chapter 6: Letting Go...................................... 49

Chapter 7: Love Shouldn't Hurt 55

Chapter 8: More than a Conqueror 63

Chapter 9: Labor of Love 71

Chapter 10: Moving Beyond the Shame 81

Poetic Justice.. 87

Conclusion 89

Survivor's Story... 90

Safety Plan 95

Resources.. 104

Author Bios... 108

Foreword

Beautifully broken is where God does His best work. One thing that I've discovered about life is bad things happen to good people and bad things happen to bad people. That's just life; it's what you do with the adversity that either makes you better or bitter. The enemy loves to keep us hostage with the shame of our secrets of abuse that we don't ever want anyone to know about. We're busy protecting people who never protected us. Afraid of our truth, we walk through life putting a Band-Aid over our scars instead of realizing we are WORTH healing.

The enemy has even polluted our thoughts by telling us at some level we deserved everything that happened to us. We were not wanted, not worth fighting for, not special, and not pretty. These are all lies from the pit of hell. Satan doesn't want us to ever wake up to the truth. WE DID NOT deserve this, and we are special. FREEDOM sets in when we finally begin to realize and admit that lack of forgiveness is holding us back. Forgiveness is our greatest gift. Forgiving someone who violated us often feels like we are pardoning a crime committed against us. If we forgive them, we may think we are saying, "You got away with what you did to me." Not true. Think about the very worst thing anyone has ever done to you. Now, think about doing something just as bad back to them. This is not healing. You see, "hurt people may continue to hurt people," but healed people help heal people. Let it go!

Listen, God is a HEALER! He didn't let the abuse and heartbreak happen to you. Through your story, He sure does plan on using it to heal millions. You made it and survived! Your scars are the tattoos that show YOU MADE IT. You may feel like you are barely getting by because the pain is still stinging; but you are here. I believe by the time you finish reading this book, you are going to feel a freedom down in your belly that you have never felt before. A promise within your belly letting you know that this too shall pass. Not only has God not forgotten about you, but He has a major promise and purpose for you. Romans 8:28 says, "That He is working ALL things together for your good." Yes, that means in every inch of your life, He is working it together to create you to come out a mighty VICTOR. You will decide NOT to let a season in your life define your whole lifetime.

I love the story of the disco ball. It is one little round object that can light up a huge room with many prism lights. It is simply breathtaking! It could not light up

6

your world if it had not been broken into a million little pieces and glued back together. Without all the cracks, light couldn't shine through. That's us! Without all the cracks and brokenness, we wouldn't shine. We are like glow sticks. We must be broken to allow our own light to shine. Wow, doesn't that really change the perspective of all the hell we have been through? Be excited and know that you will shine bright like a diamond when you release your pain and allow healing. Everyone has a story. Yours will be a BEST SELLER!

You are coming through this beautifully. Your scars are being turned into stars. Your pain is becoming your pulpit. Your test is becoming your testimony. Your mess is becoming your message. You are a game changer. Keep your heart open and be intentional about moving forward. Decide that you will not look in your rearview mirror. Resolve to use the windshield and move forward. The sky is the limit for you. God is so proud. The world needs you to make it. You are powerful. I am excited about your future!!!

Kim Jones-Pothier

Introduction

A Life Guide to Living Victoriously Over Abuse will empower you to overcome the pain from your past that may still resonate in your present. This guide will help equip you to fight through any situation by creating an Overcomers Mindset. Here you will find life-giving, transparent and inspirational messages and quotes that will empower you in your everyday life. Although this book speaks of rising above the abuse we both have personally experienced and that once held us down; this overcoming journey is for everyone. If you have ever been disappointed, discouraged, disengaged, or disheartened; this book will guide you to restoration so you can live life in absolute freedom, starting Now!

This guide will help you navigate through the hardships of life. Through our personal experiences from the authors as well as others, you will learn how to grow from the feelings of rejection, bitterness, anger, and sadness so you may live in your full potential. Step by step, you will begin to remove the layers from your past that are the residue of damage, woundedness, and even brokenness, so that you can heal again. The message of this book is this: YES, it IS possible to be restored and to return to wholeness.

This book is not a one-time read only. The reader can use this book as a tool to use in pre-recovery, after recovery, and on-going recovery.

Are you ready for a change that will leave you better and not bitter? Are you ready to disempower your past and empower your present and future? If you have answered yes, then let's begin this journey together.

We are two friends who discovered we had a common mission…to help set others free from abuse.

Kristal's perspective:

Carla and I shared the most intimate things, but never that one unspoken secret. I had her back, and she had mine. She supported me, and I supported her. Even though I always didn't get it right because of my guarded heart and my trust issues, she was number one in my eyes. Carla was my number one friend and supporter who walked with me and walked alongside me in my brokenness.

See, this was the first time I didn't have to pretend to be someone I wasn't. It was the first time that I didn't have to look around and wonder if someone was judging me. I know now that we had so much in common, it makes me wonder if our Heavenly Father had set us up to work as angels on earth. I understand now that it's a commission to help others. The mandate is to free others. I get it! I get the big picture; I get it!

Carla's perspective:

Kristal's friendship was beyond loyal. As I shared with her about my absentee father, she introduced me to a deeper relationship with our Heavenly Father as well as her own earthly father. Kristal had no idea when I met her father, Vernon, that he was to be one of the few male role models I had at that time. He showed me how a father should be to his children. He allowed me to see what it means for a male to honor, respect, and protect his family. After secretly recovering from child sexual abuse at the hands of a man that promised to be a father figure; she had no idea that introducing me to her father(s) helped to stop the leak from my heart and heal from my pain.

Throughout our friendship or should I say Sistership, she continued to stick by my side like glue sticks to paper. Through my good and bad days, she was always there. When I made wrong choices and right choices, she did not leave my side. She never judged my mistakes, and she encouraged me to do better. I am so grateful to have a true and authentic friendship that is wrapped in grace. I now know why destiny brought us together at the ripe age of 19 years old. It took us over 15 years in friendship, to start talking about our dirty little secrets. The more we started sharing, the more shame was lifted off us. It was through real life conversations that we found out what true freedom feels like and looks like. It all makes sense now. I now know why we were called together for such a time as this and for an assignment such as this!

Combined perspectives:

We knew everything about each other such as our favorite colors, the type of guys we liked and our dreams. We were the type of friends that talked about everything from nail polish, hair styles, careers, education, families, "frenemies," and everything else in between. We identified ourselves as Best Friends Forever. We shared it all including clothes, makeup, and heartbreaks. After all, that's what sisters do. Our bond was divine. We had no idea why our lives became intertwined, but God did. He had a bigger plan. He knew one day we would share the biggest secret that we kept from one another for 15 years. He knew once we shared our secrets, it would give others the power and permission to share theirs. We still can't believe we were the closest of friends, yet quietly suffering in silence behind the shame of abuse. All those years, we never compared or shared our stories. In those moments, we spent with each other, we became; unbroken, unmasked, transparent, and transformed to set others free.

We have since joined to share our pain in hopes that others will find their purpose. We are what restoration and redemption look like. What an honor it is to share our hearts with those who are also overcoming their secrets.

When you have survived hell, you are no longer afraid of the darkness. Instead, you use your torch of light to set other captives free!

Chapter 1
Silence Killers

Don't carry the burden from the mistakes that are caused by other people. It was their choice, not yours. Loose guilt and shame from your life and walk in freedom to be healed. Today walk in victory. Today take back your life. You can overcome any and everything that was sent to destroy you. Believe this!

Truth 101: I Am Stronger than my struggle. I Am More than what I have survived. My Purpose is bigger than my pain.

Kristal's Testimony: At the age of 11, I was confronted with a fear that I had never known before. I had to face my giant. I had to face my teacher in court. I finally confessed that he had sexually violated me. I was 11 years old, and I struggled with insecurity, so it took me some time to build trust with my math teacher. He allowed some of us to stay after class to get some math tutoring. One day as I was standing next to my teacher's desk, with an open hand he began to stroke my bottom. I was in shock. This one act took me back to my 4-year-old self who was violated. I remember walking away from his desk feeling as if I was frozen. I was afraid, anxious, and apprehensive. I wanted this whole thing to just go away, including the flashbacks. However, my wants were simply desires that I dreamed about.

Somehow, I knew as a child that if I didn't go through with the court proceedings, my teacher, would continue to hurt other children. I couldn't let that happen; so, I had to face my biggest source of pain. Although my parents were supportive, my classmates were not. I was bullied and ultimately transferred to another school for my protection because my abuser was the students' favorite teacher.

After a long grueling court process, my teacher was convicted. To my surprise, other students started coming forward to speak out against him as well. I vowed that day never to stay silent again. I vowed that day to stand up and speak out for myself as well as for others. I learned a valuable lesson, more than any classroom experience could have ever taught me. I learned to never suffer in silence. This experience taught me: If I speak up and speak out, I will free myself and others, too.

Today, I am living in my purpose, as the Founder of Rock Paper Scissors Foundation.

Reflection:

If you are suffering in silence, what are your biggest fears about not speaking out?

_____

_____

_____

_____

_____

_____

Write about a painful time that you can look back and see that you have overcome.

_____

_____

_____

_____

_____

_____

In what ways, can you or have you turned your pain into purpose?

_____

_____

_____

_____

_____

_____

Action: If you are suffering in silence, please contact a trusted source to help you find your voice. Healing takes time; but the first step is to talk about it. *You can't heal what you won't reveal.*

I have lost many things, but one thing I refuse to lose is my voice! My voice shatters darkness. A lost voice is lost hope. It is my greatest weapon against every fear and every enemy. If you shut up, then you will break down.

Chapter 2
Unmuted

Hurting people hurt people. Broken people break people. My hope and prayer are that I may heal so that I won't wound others AND be real enough in my healing so that others may see that overcoming is possible.

Truth 102: I couldn't STOP what happened to me, but I can STOP it from destroying me. I choose not to live another day in the shadows of my past. When I don't hide my light, I liberate others.

Carla's Testimony: I was in a domestic violence relationship that resulted in me being run over by a red four-door Caprice Classic twice in the same night, which led to an ambulance taking me to the emergency room. That unforgettable night in February was the breaking point to our already toxic relationship. In an attempt to move on from this off again and on again relationship, I fled to the military as a way of escape. I left one violent relationship, only to be assaulted again within the military. While on a temporary duty assignment, I was sexually assaulted by an officer. I was enlisted. I was so trained on how not to fraternize, but not trained on how to deal with someone who crosses the line. I didn't know how to respond.

I still can recall that night when my superior…my captain became my enemy. As a group of us were dancing on the dance floor, he came behind me and started to dance. His dance moves became more intense. Being a young recruit, I didn't know how to respond exactly. He came closer. Perhaps his ego was leading him. As I turned around, that's when I felt a feeling that I can still remember. I continued to dance, but I backed away from the feeling of being violated. As I was walking away, two large hands went up to my shirt and grabbed my most intimate parts. I was shocked! I couldn't move. As he continued with his groping, a few other officers pulled him away.

That same night, I told my female supervisor out of fear that she had seen what happened and I wondered what she might think. I foolishly thought I was going to get in trouble for fraternizing. The next day, he called out sick. My supervisor happened to take the call and confronted him. He asked to speak with me. My heart was filled with panic. I respectively answered, "Hello, Sir." He replied, "Last night, we all had a lot to drink. There isn't a problem, right?" I replied, "No, Sir." It wasn't until years later that I wondered why I never confronted him. Why didn't I speak up for myself? Why was I acting like it was no big deal? Suddenly I recalled my childhood experience of sexual abuse; I didn't speak up then either. Although I was grown enough to enlist into the military, I was still that muted little girl. I still didn't know how to articulate what was going on behind closed doors. I just knew that "it" felt wrong; but I didn't have the voice to speak. The longer I kept silent, the longer I learned how to pretend everything was just fine. But it wasn't.

During this time, I realized I had much self-work to do. I talked to trusted advisors who helped me with my healing from the pain of my past. I also cultivated healthy relationships and avoided toxic relationships by any means necessary. Deep down inside, I knew that I needed to help others break their silence, but I had to first break mine. After joining the military and doing the work of healing, I found my courage. It was the first time that I talked about "it" to others. I noticed that each time I shared my story, someone else admitted that they had also experienced some form of abuse. I remember while stationed in Japan, I had a heart-to-heart conversation with my new, dear friend Charlotte. Our normal girl talk went to real talk, which was one of the first of many more conversations to come. I shared my childhood and everything in between in total transparency and without judgment. I wasn't as alone as I once thought. This was such a freeing moment. I finally came out of the shadows and into the light. No more guilt. No more shame. Since then, I have turned my personal experience into passion by caring for children who have a history of abuse within and outside of the foster care system. I now wear the "Overcomer" badge proudly and salute those who have overcome, too. We are more than what happened to us.

Today, I am living my passion as the President of Rock Paper Scissors Foundation.

Reflection:

Discuss a time when you allowed someone to betray your trust without speaking up. What kept you from using your voice?

_____

_____

_____

_____

_____

_____

In what ways has your childhood shaped (financially, physically, emotionally, mentally) who you are today?

_____

_____

_____

_____

_____

_____

In what ways can you help others break their silence?

_____

_____

_____

_____

_____

_____

Action: If there is anyone in your past that is keeping you bound to them because you haven't forgiven them, then think of healthy ways to let them go. You may choose to tell them, write a letter without sending it, or seek assistance from a trusted source. However, you choose to free yourself it doesn't matter as long as you are "set free".

I was so busy practicing forgiving others that I forgot to forgive who matters most - Me! Sometimes the challenge isn't about forgiving others. The challenge is more about forgiving YOUrself. Don't be a harsh critic over your own weaknesses. Put your energy NOT into your mistakes but in your willingness to overcome them. Forgive YOU and move forward.

Chapter 3
Overcomers

An Overcomer is defined as someone who gains superiority over someone or something.

Truth 103: I can overcome everything I have been through. I will not bow down to the burdens of my past. Instead, I will rise above them.

Overcomers do not live in a world of denial; however, they do understand no one is exempt from pain. They are fully aware of what or who tried to bring them down and they refuse to be paralyzed by the pain of their past. We go through life without letting yesterday overshadow our tomorrow. In exchange for the badge of victimization we wear the badge of victory. Knowing how to rise above pain determines your true quality of life. Two individuals who have both experienced the same type of abuse at the same age and in the same environment can have two totally different outcomes in life. One may maneuver through life's traumas to live a successful life, while the other can struggle and live a less than desirable life. What are their differences? Meet Terri...

Testimony: From the time I was three until I was ten years old, several different men sexually molested me: mother's boyfriends, family friends, counselor at the local Boys & Girls Club, and strangers in the neighborhood. I was molested so often that I got used to it and began to believe it was "normal." Once I came of age and understood this was not right, I felt extremely violated, unprotected, and unloved by my family. I was hurt and lost. The words from my abusers, "If you ever tell anyone what happened, I will kill you," haunted me; and I never said a word. When I finally got the nerve to tell someone in my family, I was told "I was a liar," and my accounts of what happened were not true. I was angry and attempted suicide twice when I was 17 years old and then again when I was 20 years old. I felt rejected and alone, after which I fell into a deep depression which caused me to want to take my life.

I found myself as a young male adult with multiple sexual partners because I felt that I was **made for sex.** I believed this was love, and that this was how someone showed you that they cared and wanted to be with you. I associated sex with love.

When I came into a relationship with Christ and developed a great support system; I was able to overcome the hate I had for people, myself, and especially my mother. The love of God helped me forgive those who hurt me. Through reading the Bible, I realized that I could be free from all the past hurt and pain. The Word inspired me to overcome! It did not happen overnight; it took a lot of prayer, counseling, and getting up every day forgiving every person who violated me. Over time the thoughts of my past did not consume my mind or discourage my future. I used what happened to me as a vehicle to reach out to others who are experiencing or have dealt with the abuse I have encountered. As a man, it is difficult to talk about these things because it challenges my manhood and most of us are taught to be tough, so we go on in life silent, hurt, struggling, and afraid to jeopardize what in our minds seems like the little manhood we have left. I challenge everyone, especially men to speak up, you're not alone. There is help, and in time healing does occur.

I got the courage to speak out when I came across others who experienced the same abuse and were afraid to share. When I began to love myself, I was transformed into the person I was meant to be. I understood this was my testimony to help others. I dare you to choose your freedom and walk in the healing and happiness of life that is rightfully yours!

You see Terri represents both sides of the survivor spectrum. He could have continued to justifiably live his life out of his pain. He could have continued to destroy himself and those closest to him. However, Terri took what once tried to kill him and used it to murder the trauma of his past. Terri couldn't move forward until he first learned how to let go.

Reflection:

What ways have your relationships been affected by what you have experienced?

_____

_____

_____

_____

_____

_____

What can you do today that will help you cultivate and maintain healthy relationships?

_____

_____

_____

_____

_____

_____

Action: Choose to surround yourself with healthy people. Healthy relationships do not cause physical harm, sexual abuse, and or manipulative behaviors. Refuse to give any more time and attention to negative relationships.

Once you find yourself forgiving, you may find yourself needing to heal again. Life throws us curve balls; but it's up to us to catch each ball and not stop running! Don't give up no matter what comes your way!

Chapter 4
Outliving Your Pain

Truth 104: Wasted pain means hurting in vain. I will promote my pain to the position of purpose. I will use what I've been through to help someone else.

Pain isn't always visible to the human eye, but if you look close enough, you can see it in the way someone behaves or "doesn't" behave. Pain can have a crippling effect on us all. It can cause us to stop dead in our tracks while we frantically try and nurse our wounds. Some say that time heals everything; however, try telling that to the adult whose childhood stood still after being violated. Time is not a mystery medication that heals all things. There are plenty of people who have died in pain and lived to be very old. The only remedy for pain is addressing it. There are some who will cover up their pain by being in multiple relationships, focusing on overachievement, are addicted to substances, and so much more.

If pain were a color, it would be described as camouflage because it is not easily revealed to the human eye. Pain has the ability to blend in with the surroundings of its host. However, if you watch close enough, you will see the destruction that it leaves behind.

To outlive your pain, you must be committed to restoration and recovery. You must be willing to be uncomfortable as you face truths, and cleanse yourself of the emotional damage someone caused you. As ironic as it may seem, you must be willing to embrace the pain to heal. What does outliving pain look like? Meet Dee...

Testimony: I was molested by several people, both male and female, between the ages of four to twelve years old. And at the age of 14, I was raped on a date in my high school parking lot. The sexual abuse caused me to have a tremendous amount of guilt and shame.

I hid those terrible secrets for close to 40 years. I remember every incident; and even today I occasionally get triggered by certain smells, places, and images.

Growing up, I was raised by a very loving single mom, and we lived in both Seattle and the Bay Area. To everyone, I seemed to be energetic, talkative, and a bit stubborn; but was an overall a happy little girl. On the inside, I was sad. I didn't feel like I could trust anyone and I had an overwhelming need to please everyone.

At 14 years old, I was raped in my high school parking lot. After the rape, I couldn't handle the secrets that I had buried deep within. The assault triggered the memories of being sexually abused from the ages of 4 to 12 years old. Years of trauma led me to control the only thing that I could control, which was my food intake. I spiraled emotionally out of control and developed an eating disorder, bulimia. I would binge and use diet pills, laxatives, and restricted my food intake to stay thin.

As much as I thought I was managing my life at the time, I continued to spiral out of control. I struggled off and on with an eating disorder, and I placed my value and self-worth on whatever the number on the scale said. My compulsive behaviors controlled me. At school, I was an overachieving perfectionist, but away from school, I was very promiscuous, and occasionally used drugs and alcohol to numb my pain.

My life turned around when I was a freshman in college. At the age of 19, I became pregnant and a single mom to a beautiful baby boy. During this time, I began attending church and became a Christian. For the first time in my life, I had a peace of mind and hope for my future.

After struggling for 32 years with my eating disorder, I can say today that I am not active in the disorder. I am in therapy; and attend recovery meetings, all while healing from the pain of childhood sexual abuse.

I believe everyone has a calling and a purpose and that you can use any negative situation and turn it around to be positive. My passion is working with students ranging from middle school age to millennials. I am currently the Assistant to the Director in the Office of Student Engagement at Sacramento State University's College of Business. The best part of my job is helping students grow personally and professionally. I take pride in investing in other people's lives; and I'm driven by encouraging and uplifting those around me.

Being part of Rock Paper Scissors (RPS) Foundation has given me an amazing opportunity to let people know that they are not alone, and that healing is possible. Being an advocate, it brings awareness about how to empower victims of abuse. I am building an RPS "Break the Silence" community in Northern California; and we are giving people hope.

Reflections:

What have you done to try and camouflage your pain?

_____

_____

_____

_____

_____

_____

What can you do today to continue your healing journey?

_____

_____

_____

_____

_____

_____

Action: There are trusted counselors who will walk out this courageous journey with you; but you must be willing to make the call. There are close confidantes who can support you; but you must be willing to reveal what needs to be healed. Healing doesn't come without hard work. Reach out to someone to assist with your healing.

Forgiveness is a gift to you, not the other person. It frees you from the power that would otherwise keep you handcuffed to them and the pain they've caused. Forgiveness doesn't mean the other person deserves to be forgiven. Forgiveness means that you deserve it.

Chapter 5
Redeemed from Regret

Truth 105: I must forgive myself on a continuous basis. Yes, I have made some mistakes; but I am not a mistake.

Guilt and shame only serve one purpose. It robs you of today's peace. Too many times, we are often overly critical of ourselves and others because we are trying to overcompensate for our past. We sometimes use a strict lens of judgment when it comes to ourselves and others. To truly heal, we must lift the weight of guilt and shame off us. How can this seemingly unsurmountable task be done? Meet Joe...

Testimony: Surely, she wouldn't marry a man that had been raped and molested by two of his sisters. My anger and hurt are how I justified touching three innocent victims myself in my early years. I know now that hurt people, hurt people! I didn't go as far as rape because that was the worst pain I ever felt. However, my anger towards women is what fueled my actions "regret." Hiding my shame, guilt, pain, rage, self- hatred, and running from God, was easy at first. But as time went on, the weight of my abuse became unbearable. "Hurts" developed into "Habits" that became "Hang-ups." I tried eating to hide my feelings, and that worked, for a while. So, then I consumed myself with playing Madden NFL football video games, this allowed me to temporarily ignore the pain.

Sixteen years ago, my marriage started with a lie "regret." I told my wife I was a virgin. Imagine how miserable my marriage was! I was unable to say I love you to the one woman that could touch me without me freezing with panic and fear. However, my anger and hatred toward women were what attracted me to porn. The degrading and belittling of women fueled my rage, and pretty soon I had a one-night stand. I started going to massage parlors to fulfill my need for love, but it was still not enough. Then I went looking for prostitutes, still not enough. Then strip clubs…nothing could quench my pain and my thirst for love, forgiveness, and grace. Finally, on Mother's Day, my wife learned of my secrets, and I couldn't lie anymore. My walls caved in as the truth poured out of my mouth. Jesus was already starting a work in me. But just as I had feared, she packed up and took the kids. She said, with tears in her eyes, "I'll be back in a week, and you need to be gone." I don't care where you go just don't be here." At this point, I felt helpless and hopeless and decided to make the 5th attempt on my life. From the ages of 19-36 years old I tried and failed to hang myself. Each time the rope broke or the tree branch broke. Each time I knew that it was Jesus telling me it's not my time.

I knew Jesus had been working on my heart and I needed help. I knew Jesus was working on me because my heart would race, palms sweaty, and the conviction of knowing right from wrong. I didn't understand it at first, but I was reminded of something from my childhood. Luckily my mom made me go to church, so I remembered being taught that suicide is the unforgivable sin. I knew I had hit rock bottom with no hope and no light to be seen if I committed this act of sin. When my wife returned, I was still there. I begged for an ounce of hope of saving our marriage, but she said no. So, I begged her to teach me how to pray, she then took my hands and said, "Close your eyes, pretend that the hands you are holding are the hands of Jesus and just talk to him. Tell him everything that is in your heart. Ask him to forgive you of all your sins. Ask him for help." So, I sobbed and cried out to God and talked to Jesus for about ten minutes. I begged my wife to go with me to church the next day, and she agreed.

I have been a member of a church for 14 years, but I didn't KNOW Jesus. That changed in one day. I MET Jesus by going to church and reading the Bible., and discovered HIS love, grace, hope, and forgiveness. The best thing about this day was my 15yr old that had been praying for daddy since the age of five was sitting beside mommy to witness the power of prayer being answered. My wife said, "I'm proud of you, but this doesn't change anything." I was ok with this because so many times I told her I would change. I knew she had to see it to believe it this time. I believe that with God all things are possible. With constant prayers and communication over several weeks, we had "True Confession" sessions, and for the first time in our marriage, we were totally and completely honest with one another. Because as she will tell you, she was not totally innocent either. She had things that needed to be forgiven because she too has been caring around Hurts, Habits, and Hang -ups. We forgave ourselves and each other by taking it one day at a time. We have grown closer to each other because we have grown closer to God.

I thought I had forgiven my sisters, but God showed me I was still hiding and holding anger towards them. One night in church, the service was amazing, and yet the only words I remember were "Maybe it's a family member that has hurt you, and you need to make amends." Wow!!! The rage and anger that flowed through my blood were like nothing I can remember. I said, "God, I don't understand. I forgave them. Why am I still angry?" God said, "Son, would I have forgiven you if you had not asked?" I said, "No." All I could say is, "Wow" again!!! So about three weeks later I called them and truly forgave them. My wife, my family, and I are happier now than we have ever been. My eating habits are improving. My sex/porn addiction doesn't control me anymore. It's still a constant battle, but with God, I'm winning! All the glory belongs to God. I believe that "With God nothing is impossible!"

Reflection:

What negative past experience is still robbing you of today's peace?

_____

_____

_____

_____

_____

_____

What can you do to let go of guilt, shame, and regret?

_____

_____

_____

_____

_____

Action: Whenever guilt, shame, and regret attempt to resurface in your life, remind yourself that you have been fully forgiven. Remind yourself that your "then" is not your "now."

Whenever you find yourself struggling with forgiveness, remind yourself that forgiveness is free.

Chapter 6
Letting Go

Truth 106: When I dwell on old negative thoughts, experiences, and relationships too long, I will find myself re-wounded again. What could have...should have...did not happen, and there is nothing that I can do about that. A huge part of letting go is to not live in the past so that I am able to sail into my future.

Healing from betrayal can be an uphill process. Each step forward can try to take your breath away. Triggers seem to be ever present. The same relationships that used to make you smile have now caused great grief. What do you do when those closest to you are the cause of your pain? Forgiving a stranger is one thing; but how do you forgive those whom you trusted with all of your heart? Is it possible to ever forgive the underserving? Meet Chelsea...

Testimony: I wasn't walking down a dark alley. I wasn't kidnapped. I wasn't followed by some lunatic and then attacked. That's not at all how it happened to me. He was my friend. Someone I'd hung out with, laughed with, talked with, and ate with.

I was in his city working, and he asked me to stay the night with him. I told him, "No because I don't want to have sex with you." He said he understood our friendship and knew I wasn't into him "like that." After a night of drinking and having a good time with a group of friends, I was incredibly inebriated, and I passed out. The next morning, I woke up in his hotel room, fully clothed, and feeling fine. The day continued as it normally would. Got up, got dressed, and was ready for the work day ahead. Later, in the day, he walked up to me admiring a bite mark he'd put on my neck (which I never knew was there) and followed up by giving me a play by play of what he'd sexually done to me. At that moment, my heart broke because he assured me that he knew I didn't want to have sex with him. We were "just friends"; and he wouldn't try it. It was confusing to me because I didn't remember anything. Not a thing. How did I even end up with him after previously telling him no? I felt devastated, dirty, embarrassed, and betrayed. I basically succumbed to pretty much every negative emotion you can think of.

After taking some days to process how I felt, I expressed my hurt and anger to him. I told him how he violated me, that he crossed a line that was never to be crossed without my conscious permission. He was very apologetic, assuring me he never meant to hurt me and that he went too far. Our friendship meant too much to him, and he didn't want to lose that. We agreed that we would never talk about it or tell anyone. So, I moved on with my life. Not having any recollection of that dreadful night, allowed me to put it so far in the back of my mind where I almost forgot.

Months later it came out that he'd been telling people that he "smashed" me. Devastation once again was what I felt because I was faced with a truth that I tried so hard to forget. And yet, here it was, staring me in the face. It felt like my world came crashing down on me, and crying was my only escape. Until I started counseling, which helped me tremendously, I realized I'd been blaming myself for an event that wasn't my fault. It wasn't my fault. IT WASN'T MY FAULT!! It was his. After about three years of no communication, he reached out to me, requesting my forgiveness. As impossible as it once seemed, I forgave him. At that moment, I decided I was no longer going to be a "victim." I was no longer going to wear an invisible cloak of shame. And forgiveness was the only way to truly walk in my freedom, I'm glad to say that since that day, I've been free. "Truly unbroken."

Reflection:

What or who do you need to let go of?

_____

_____

_____

_____

_____

_____

How will your life look after you decide to let that something or someone go?

_____

_____

_____

_____

_____

_____

Action: Read these words out loud "I am letting go of everything and everyone who is not called to my purposeful present."

Don't quit. Don't give up. Don't turn back. The road that you are journeying on is no reflection of your final destination. Sometimes you have to press through to breakthrough. Victory is yours. Keep pressing. Keep pushing. Keep believing. Keep the finish line in mind. You can't change history, but you can impact your destiny.

Chapter 7
Love Shouldn't Hurt

Truth 107: My self-worth is defined by me and me alone. I will never give someone else the power to give me my identity. They are not my Creator!

We were born for relationships. It is natural to crave the affection and the matchless bond from someone else. However, what happens when that natural craving has become your biggest curse and a dependency? What happens when you are drawn to toxic people who poison your soul? How do you untie the soul tie? Meet Ann...

Testimony: As a child, I always wanted the perfect family. I wanted a husband, the white picket fence, the dog, and two children. This is what I wanted. I was a "good girl." I didn't lose my virginity until I was 17. By then I went through a stage of knowing what sex was and I knew I liked it, but I didn't know what a healthy relationship looked like.

I lost my parents trust, was kicked out of our home, and I was lost. I became pregnant, and I wanted to be a stay at home mother, but my boyfriend left while I was pregnant. I found out there were four other girls pregnant by him the same time I was. After I had my son, I felt that I was supposed to be alone and I believed that I deserved all the bad in the world because I was such a horrible person before I had my son. See, I used to use drugs, and I was an exotic dancer in the club.

I got in my first abusive relationship when my son was about three months old. He was a drunk, and he would get extremely violent. I stayed with him because I wanted a family so bad. He had taken on the responsibility of my son as his own, and when he was sober, he was a great person. One day when my son was almost three years old, and he was very, very drunk, he began hitting me and slamming my head into a wall. My son comes out the room crying and saying, "Daddy" please don't hurt "Mommy." He then turned and smacked my son across the living room. After that, he had to go. The abuse didn't stop there. When he would see me in the street, he would stop me and begin to choke me in front of everybody. We weren't even together.

My second relationship was also abusive, that was about a year after the first one. This guy was addicted to meth, and I didn't know at first. I figured out that I had a tendency to want to fix people. I wanted to bring men into my life who needed me when in reality I was the one who was co-dependent. The strong desire I had for a family caused me to seek dysfunctional and abusive relationships.

The second relationship was a lot worse than the first one. When he would get high on meth, the abuse would begin. The types of abuse that would happen where, he would slam my head into the TV, punch holes in the wall, and put dents in the refrigerator. One time he bit me so hard that it caused an abscess in my arm. While all of this was going on, my dad was in the hospital dying. I left him after my dad passed.

Six months later, I got involved in another relationship. We had sex, and I ended up getting pregnant. He said if I didn't get an abortion he was going to beat the baby out of me. I got the abortion, and he still beat me.

The abuse wasn't just physical abuse. I have dealt with verbal abuse and mental abuse my whole life. I'm not good enough, I'm not smart enough, I'm worthless, I'm fat, I will never amount to anything, and I don't deserve to live was how I felt. I got some help, and now I realize those words are not true. I started a support group. I realized that I am NOT any of those things. I am NOT what these men have told me. I am NOT worthless. Yes, I struggle. Yes, I could be better, but I know I will not be hit again. Right after I started my group, I thought I had found a good relationship, but again it turned to violence.

This time I didn't give him a second chance. He hit me, and he had to go. He begged to come back, and I finally put my foot down and said no. The violence and abuse towards women are the most horrendous things in the world. I wish abusive men would realize women are valuable. I am valuable. I still get weak and think negatively; I feel myself crying because I am alone, I still feel like it's my fault sometimes. Every relationship that I get into violence happens. Maybe I'm the one that needs it. Maybe it is my fault. Maybe if I didn't say some of the things I said, I wouldn't get hit. Maybe if I just was quiet and let them speak in rage instead of defending myself maybe I wouldn't get hit.

My dad never hit my mom; I never saw abuse growing up, so how did I adopt this behavior? How in the world did I let it get to this? How am I going to teach my son the right way if all he sees is men hitting his mom? Questions I ask myself every single day, every time I look at the scars. Every time I look at the holes in my wall, I remember the bad things. But somehow, I always go and get a man with the same tendencies. Abuse has no color. Abusers are military men, businessman, and thugs. So maybe it is me, but I know one thing; if it was me, it's not going to be me anymore.

Reflection:

What have you allowed or done "in the name of love" that has had a negative affect?

_____

_____

_____

_____

_____

_____

Describe healthy love.   What are some ways that you can attract this type of love into your life?

_____

_____

_____

_____

_____

_____

Action: Read these words out loud "I do not have to settle. I am worthy of healthy love." Begin to start the process of severing unhealthy ties.

We start hearing negative things so much that we believe them. The truth is that words that hurt you don't have to define you!

Chapter 8
More than a Conqueror

Truth 108: I cannot conquer what I don't confront. I cannot confront what I don't identify.

There are some things we don't want to deal with. We want to leave those secrets under lock and key. Yes, it is scary, uncomfortable, and downright painful; but there is freedom on the other side. However, if we don't deal with the issues of our past, then how can we truly move forward? Meet Gretchen...

Testimony: I'm sure you've heard this many times. I'm sure you've read about abuse before. I'm sure that you may even know someone or you are someone who knows about abuse first hand. The thing is, you haven't heard it from me. My story is my own.

Where do I begin? You see, my story is a little different. I've never had to endure the pain of sexual abuse or assault. I've never been a victim of human trafficking. However, I have been a victim of verbal, mental, and domestic abuse. This isn't easy to tell. It's not easy for me to tell you that my mother, who I love and miss so much...verbally and mentally abused me. It's not easy for me to tell you that my mother, the one who was supposed to instill values, confidence and self-love in me, was doing the very opposite. She told me that I was ugly, treating me as if I wasn't her own, never telling me that she loved me, and making me take care of my siblings long before she got sick. She would leave me alone at home on many occasions with my siblings while she ran the streets. I hated myself, and I didn't want to live. I can remember as a teenager taking pills to end it all, then out of the blue, a "friend" called because she sensed something was wrong. When I told her what I had done, she and her grandmother came to pick me up. They helped me get some help with my addiction. I can remember always looking in the mirror repeating these words over and over, "I HATE MYSELF!"

Fast forward some years later, my mother passed away, and my siblings and I moved in with our grandparents. They were the best grandparents in the world! Why didn't I run to them instead of staying with my mother? The answer, because I wasn't leaving my siblings in a situation where they'd have to feel and endure everything that I did from our mother. At that point, I became my brothers and sisters' keeper!

I was in a relationship during the time of my mom's passing. Let me say I "thought" this was the best thing that could've happened to me! He asked me to be his wife; I said, "yes!" But I didn't pay attention to the signs. Once outside of a church while in a car, he wrapped his hand around my neck out of anger. It happened again the day before our wedding. This time I received a swollen lip and hands wrapped around my neck. I covered up the evidence and married him anyway. I believed that he would never do it again.

Years into the marriage, children were born, and the abuse continued. He cheated on me for years, but somehow, he would twist it around and accuse me. I got accused of cheating. I began to isolate myself from my family. All I did was go to his family's church. Everything in my life was toxic! I lost myself; I didn't know who I was; and I didn't love this man anymore. The biggest mistake I ever made was convincing myself to stay with this man for the sake of the kids because they witnessed the violence and pain! Fear had me stuck as he told me frequently that, "No one else would ever want me because I have three kids." I was made to believe...I WAS NOTHING.

Suicide was my way out, or so I thought. I tried to end it on several occasions. But I didn't succeed right away. It seems that I'd always wake up the following day. I needed help but with me not having a job and with three kids to support I felt shameful and it kept me from seeking help. I was a stay at home mom, who was fearful in my own home and lost. I cried to God like never before, asking him to show me a way out of this madness. I believe God gave me strength because I got tired of the abuse. I no longer wanted my kids to see me in this state.

About five or six years ago, I was set free but not before I had to get nine stitches! For me, this was my rock bottom. I had to get an order of protection and then I filed for divorce and took my life back by the grace of God.

I was not willing to be a victim any longer. It was hard getting back on my feet, but it was worth the peace of mind and the peace of knowing my children would see me get better.

I have a lot of physical scars, but I am grateful that I'm able to share just a glimpse of it to help someone else. Just know that you DO NOT have to stay, you DO NOT have to settle. If you see the signs, get out before it's too late. Do not stay with someone who is controlling your every move, who does not want you to have friends and verbally abuses you. These are all warning signs. Get out before you're unable to. Get out for your children, but most of all get out for yourself. How did I recover from all of this? I didn't go to an actual therapist, and there's nothing wrong with doing that if you choose to. As for me, I went to the only therapist I know...Jesus! He brought me out! He restored me and He healed me. I'm a survivor, I am a conqueror, and this is... My Story!

Reflection:

What was one of the hardest situations that you ever had to conquer?

_____

_____

_____

_____

_____

_____

If you were able to overcome the situation that you listed, what is stopping you from conquering the other situations that you still need to overcome?

_____

_____

_____

_____

_____

Action: Read these words out loud, "Whatever comes my way, I will be able to confront and conquer that too."

Don't be so loyal to others that you fail to be loyal to yourself. You cannot pour out of a vessel that can't hold any water.

Chapter 9
Labor of Love

Truth 9: You will have to love yourself and others through tough times.

It is not easy loving ourselves as well as others while in the cycle of abuse. At times, you will be angry, hurt, disappointed, and so forth. However, love must remain. What happens when you are running on empty, and you have no more love to give? What do you do when you see your loved one in the vicious cycle of abuse, and you have done all that you can? Meet this Warrior Mom...

Testimony: A Mother's Worst Nightmare

It was the most unimaginable nightmare in living Hell any mother could think of or comprehend. The day you realize your sweet precious daughter has been lured into the ugly world of human trafficking. She was now a victim! My world fell apart in front of me, and my life was changed forever. I became extremely depressed, suffered severe anxiety, and suffered a major mental breakdown.

Toppling over furniture; coffee and dining room table decorations, and firewood flew around the entire living room. Anything that could move was an article for me to throw! Behind the disaster was a suffering mother who was uneducated, fearful, afraid, scared, confused, frustrated, and worried about the danger my child was in.

As I lay among the firewood in a ball curled up on the floor sobbing uncontrollably, I prayed: Dear God Please Help Me! Please, someone, help me!

I would not return to work for a month, as I was unable to work or function. That was when my journey began. I was an emotional wreck. I started drinking to erase my sorrow, but that just led me down more of a dark emotional path. One day after lying on the floor I called my son and told him I needed to get some help, and that was the day I realized that I had to fight! I had to fight for my life first before I could help my daughter. Fearful and afraid, accepting my reality, I took the step forward to learn how to best help and save my daughter. The next month was devoted to educating myself by seeking help, advice, information, and knowledge from any person or organization well-versed in the awful world of trafficking. I had become a sponge, soaking up any information anyone could teach me. I learned of the control, power, and manipulation the pimp had over my daughter. In my learning process, I met some truly wonderful people and organizations who helped me become strong again. They gave me the tools to cope, prayed with me and stayed by my side all through this terrible journey in Hell.

It all started when my daughter was lured to California in the summer of 2011. With the first call from my daughter, "MOM" as she screamed in a voice of terror no mother wants to hear. "He is prostituting me and forcing me to walk the track!" Then "click". She was gone. She would go on to be raped, beat, have her eyebrows burned off with a lighter and her face slashed with a razor blade five times! She was beaten until her face was unrecognizable, and then tossed out of the car naked, and left to die. She would end up in the hospital, twice on her death bed! She was under the control of the ugliest monster, the Pimp; and he would beat her, manipulate her, and instill fear in her to control her every move. She would do what she was forced to, to protect herself. That was her first experience with a pimp. This torture and hell went on for three months.

Then came the second pimp. He held my daughter at gunpoint for three nights in a local hotel room as she was forced to have sex with Johns as he hid in the bathtub. Manipulating and controlling her every move!

My world was falling apart as the third pimp from hell entered my daughter's life. He lured and manipulated her, used physical, and emotional abuse and threats to keep her working. My daughter was once again a victim of human trafficking. She was forced by him with fraud and coercion, to keep working as a prostitute for his financial gain. She was in his control! She was trafficked and transported through five different states!

I learned the tactics the pimps would use. I learned about disposable phones, advertising, escort names, and about "Backpage." The ugly internet site would become my new obsession! Sadly, I learned and experienced what my daughter had to do in that awful world. I tried to save her from it, but she would return to her pimps over and over again. I was told she would return to her pimp about seven times before she would fully escape "the life." Though she was not physically with the pimp, he still had control of her mind and was able to control and manipulate her heart. She believed that she was in love with her pimp and that he loved her. The love that she thought was real was how he controlled her. He made her believe that what she was doing was ok.

No mother wants to see her child's half naked pictures on the internet, selling her body for sex for a pimp! It was devastating and painful to see these pictures of my daughter. My heart was in my stomach, and my eyes filled with tears. I was sick! It soon became my only means to locate my daughter. To see her current pictures and postings was the only way I knew if she was dead or alive!

Through all this time the contacts in my phone became many police officers and detectives from different states. I was a mother on a mission. A mother living in hell, using all my resources to find my daughter and bring her home safely! I was blessed to work with a couple of wonderful detectives who continued to support and assist me. With their help, knowledge, care and concern along with the police force, they would help me to bring my daughter home!

She turned two of her pimps into the police. I was so proud of her! Working with the police, detectives, and prosecutors, she was able to have the pimp who held her at gunpoint arrested. My daughter worked with detectives and the police to set her pimp up. She called him and told him she wanted to meet with him, and he agreed. He had no idea my daughter would show up that night. Well, he showed up at the meeting place, and they arrested him! I was a nervous wreck, but when they arrested him I was relieved! He went to court and was sentenced ten months in jail.

She eventually turned in the pimp who trafficked her through five states; after a long, scary, fearful 14 months! I was now the mother completing this awful mission to put these monsters in prison. My daughter was wonderful. I was so proud of her for turning him in and getting him off the street as well as saving other girls from him. This pimp was sent to Federal Court, with a Grand Jury. My daughter testified for three long grueling days, having to relive all of the torture she endured. I also testified as well. Sitting in the witness stand, glaring at the pimp and hating him as I was telling my story of the hell and torture he put me and my daughter through. I was extremely fearful, nervous, and relieved that he was going to suffer and be punished. He was found guilty of Trafficking and Prostitution. He was sentenced to 16 1/2 years in prison!

I was overjoyed and relieved. The nightmare was over, and justice was served!! My ugly Nightmare from Hell was over four years later! I survived that which I never thought I would! A mother living in such terror, fright, and in the unknown, was such an awful, scary experience. I got through it with the help and support of so many wonderful people, trafficking organizations, and law enforcement. I could not have done it without them. I am so grateful to them all! I am So Blessed!! I am so Thankful!

I am proud to say my daughter is now doing well and thriving. She is home, living with me, and attending beauty college! She is happy, she is at peace, and has turned her life around! She is strong; she is a success; she is a survivor!

Reflections:

Who are you waiting for to be free of abuse?

_____

_____

_____

_____

_____

_____

What ways can you show love even if they are not ready to leave their troubling situation?

_____

_____

_____

_____

_____

_____

Action: Be sure to practice self-care while you are caring for someone else. When we are depleted, we have nothing to give. You can be a voice of love when they need it most by practicing self-care.

Be patient with You. We are all a work in progress. Perfection is just an unattainable illusion. Give yourself room for error and depend on grace to transform you.

Chapter 10
Moving Beyond the Shame

Truth 10: I am not a victim. I am more than a survivor. I am a winner and champion of my life! I never gave up and kept fighting until victory was the only option.

Those we expect to protect us and love us can also be the ones that hurt us. This truth is a sobering reality for many. However, how can you move forward when you share the same bloodline, memories, and bonding ties with your offender? Meet Candy...

Testimony: At six years old, I was just a young girl who loved to play pretend with my dolls and ride my bike all around the neighborhood with my friends. Both parents in the home were engulfed in work and trying to make ends meet. I was innocent and oblivious to what harm was. At that time, I was one of three children. My older brother and sister were six and seven years older than me. Imagine trying to keep up with teenagers. When my parents would leave home at night due to work, my older siblings would sneak and flip the cable switch to mischievously partake in viewing X-rated shows on the television. Me, not knowing any better I would catch them watching and they would shush me to my room and swear me to secrecy. This went on for a long time. I didn't quite understand what I saw on the television. I had no clue that it was sowing a seed that would later come back to haunt me. My parents worked a lot and would leave me in the care of my siblings. This particular day my sister was not home, and it was just my brother and me. He called me to his room and what happened next is a memory I care not to relive. Afterward, I remember feeling confused as to why my brother would ask me to do those things to him. I was sworn to secrecy. I thought it was normal. Soon after, it happened to me again with another boy in the neighborhood. And again, I wondered if this was normal?! Being molested?!

I began acting out because I started to feel disgusted and eventually I began to talk back. Fast forward years later, that seed of abuse was just festering in me. As a teenager, I became very promiscuous. The seed had become a full grown oak tree by the time I reached adulthood. Not understanding why my sense of love and security had been warped by a seed sown decades before, I had to get to the bottom of it. I remember being at a church event and they did a call for freedom for anyone who had been molested. My parents were there, but I did not care. I had to free myself from the secret pain and shame I had been carrying. This later sparked challenging dialogue between my parents and me, but I had to stand firm in the truth of what I experienced. It took years for me to forgive my brother whom I had never personally confronted.

You see, as a growing teenager he had issues with aggression, he was in and out of youth homes; and he eventually spent most of his adult life in the prison system. So, for me, I had to come to grips with possibly not receiving an apology or him not owning up to what he did. That took years and many prayers and conversations with God.

Through time, God healed my heart and removed the shame of what I experienced. I felt God leading me to scriptures that affirmed that I was fearfully and wonderfully made. I'm grateful that today I no longer stand under a cloud of what happened to me as a child. I'm now a woman whose life is better because I know who I am and I don't have to accept anything that would bring shame to my virtue. I'm whole, and I'm free!

Reflection:

What would you tell the younger child in you that has experienced something devastating? If you have not ever experienced something devastating in your childhood, what would you tell another child that has?

_____
_____
_____
_____
_____
_____

What can you gain by moving forward?

_____
_____
_____
_____
_____
_____

Action: Envision your life in absolute freedom from past misfortunes. Write down what that looks like. Do one thing today that will bring you closer to true freedom.

My tears are not a sign of my weakness. In fact, my tears are my liquid strength. My tears are the healing waters that are drawn from the well of my soul. My tears remind me that I can still feel; and if I can still feel then I can still heal.

Poetic Justice

In the corners of your mind, you thought you had me...

Doom and gloom are what you presumed, but He said in Him I have life in full bloom.

I claim a life of shear vitality and erasing the shame and doubt of her story's fatality.
My premature life was aborted six years too late. But my spirit held on to the promise of my fate.

I am the head and not the tail. I am above and not beneath your hell.
The little girl in me was raped by your naivety?

But, today I'm walking in the promise God wills for me.
Rock, Paper, Scissors best out of three. But I come armed with the undefeated Trinity.
I take back the joy you bared arms and staked out of me.

God replaced it with purpose, and my testimony is David slaying your Goliath attempts to break me.
You preyed on me. He prayed for me. Saying, forgive them, Father, for they know not what they do. Holding your children's innocence for ransom but the enemy's debts are past due.
So, I get out your boxed in view of me. I pray you gain His vision to see clearly.

Even Paul was redeemed, and his blackened heart was
wiped clean.
So, yes, it's not too late even for you. He can heal the
hurts that haunt you too.

~T. Samaria

Conclusion

What does acceptance look like to you?

Is it working hard to be like everyone else? Or are we putting aside our true selves all for acceptance? These negative messages of perception have a way of creeping in through words like, "Don't do that; Don't say that; Don't wear that; They won't like that." These are our inner battles that we can become victorious over. These negative perceptions are the struggles within when you feel acceptance is not yours. When you feel you're not good enough. When your insecurities have control. That thirst for acceptance is strong when you don't love yourself. Acceptance of self should be the goal. Loving your weirdness, awkwardness, corniness, and silliness. It's loving your true self, despite what your family thinks. Despite what your friends think. Despite what society says. BE YOU, ALL OF YOU! That's true acceptance. Do what you want; say what you want; and wear what you want. Accept who you are, ALL OF YOU! You are amazing. You are important. You are beautiful, smart, wanted, and needed. Lovely, You, are brilliant, Beautifully made, and Perfectly flawed. Acceptance is not in others; Acceptance is in YOU!

~Catrina

Survivor's Story

One voice became 100 voices. 100 voices became thousands of voices. Together, we take a stand to speak out and fight against injustices. We promise to use our pain for a greater purpose. We vow not to live in silence. We keep our commitment of being Silence Killers! Will you join the movement and lend us your voice?

We understand the power of speaking out. We invite you to embrace this undeniable power today. Join us in breaking the silence. Write your story below. Then we would love for you to share it with us!

_____

Survivor's Story (Print your Name)

_____

_____

_____

_____

_____

_____

_____
_____
_____
_____
_____
_____
_____
_____
_____
_____
_____
_____
_____
_____
_____
_____
_____
_____
_____
_____
_____
_____
_____
_____
_____
_____
_____
_____
_____
_____
_____
_____
_____

How have You Overcome?

_____

_____

_____

_____

_____

_____

Domestic Violence Safety Plan

A safety plan is a personalized, practical plan that includes ways to remain safe while in a potentially dangerous relationship, planning to leave, or after you leave. Safety planning involves how to cope with emotions, tell friends and family about the abuse, take legal action and more.

Safety Plan:

- Seek Out Supportive People: A caring presence such as a trusted friend or family member can help create a calm atmosphere to think through difficult situations and allow for you to discuss potential options.

- Make a plan for how you are going to leave, including where you're going to go, and how to cover your tracks. Make one plan for if you have time to prepare to leave the home. Make another plan for if you have to leave the home in a hurry.

- If possible, have a phone accessible at all times and know what numbers to call for help. Know where the nearest public phone is located. Know the phone number to your local shelter. If your life is in danger, call the police.

- Let trusted friends and neighbors know of your situation and develop a plan and visual signal for when you need help Teach your children how to get help. Instruct them not to get involved in the violence between you and your partner. Plan a code word to signal to them that they should get help or leave the house.

- Practice how to get out safely. Practice with your children. Plan for what you will do if your children tells your partner of your plan or if your partner otherwise finds out about your plan.

- Keep weapons like guns and knives locked away and as inaccessible as possible.

- Make a habit of backing the car into the driveway and keeping it fueled. Keep the driver's door unlocked and others locked for a quick escape.

- Create several plausible reasons for leaving the house at different times of the day or night.

- Have a bag packed that you can easily grab- with clothing, medications, spare car and house keys, important phone numbers, copies of important legal papers. You can hide the bag at home or keep it at a trusted friend's home.

- Try to set money aside for when you do leave. If the abuser controls the household money, this might mean that you can only save a few dollars per week; the most important thing is that you save whatever amount you can that will not tip off the abuser and put you in further danger. You can ask trusted friends or family members to hold money for you so that the abuser cannot find it and/or use it.

- Leave when the abuser will least expect it. This will give you more time to get away before the abuser realizes that you are gone.

- If you have time to call the police before leaving, you can ask the police to escort you out of the house as you leave. You can also ask them to be "on call" while you're leaving, in case you need help. Not all police precincts will help you in these ways, but you may want to ask your local police station if they will.

Human Trafficking Safety Plan

In some cases, leaving or attempting to leave a trafficking situation may increase the risk of violence. It is important to trust your judgment when taking steps to ensure your safety.

- If you are ever in immediate danger, the quickest way to access help is to call 9-1-1.

- If you are unsure of your current location, try to determine any indication of your locality such as street signs or landmarks outside of the residence/place of employment or newspapers/magazines/mail that may have the address listed.

- If it is safe to go outside, see if the address is listed anywhere on the building.

- If there are people nearby and it is safe to speak with them, ask them about your current location.

- Plan an escape route or exit strategy and rehearse it if possible.

- Prepare a bag with any important documents/items and a change of clothes.

- Think about your next steps after you leave the situation.

- Keep a written copy of important numbers on you at all times in case your phone is taken or destroyed at any point. Memorize important hotline numbers if possible.

- Contact trusted friends/relatives to notify them or to ask for assistance if you feel comfortable.

- Contact the National Human Trafficking Resource Center (NHTRC) 24-hour hotline at 1-888-3737-888 to obtain local referrals for shelter or other social services and support.

- If you would like assistance from law enforcement, you may also contact the NHTRC to report your situation and/or connect with specialized local law enforcement referrals. Please note: if you are ever in immediate danger, contact 9-1-1 first.

During violent/explosive situations, try to avoid dangerous rooms if at all possible.

- Examples of Dangerous Rooms: knives, sharp utensils, pots, garage tools, sharp objects, bathroom (hard surfaces, no exits), basement (hard surfaces, no exits), rooms where weapons are kept and rooms without an exit.

- Examples of Safer Rooms: front room, yard or apartment hallway where a neighbor might see or hear an incident.

- Develop a special signal (lights flickering on and off, code word, code text message, hand signal, etc.) to use with a trusted neighbor, relative, friend or service provider to notify them that you are in danger.

- If you have children who are also in a human trafficking situation, explain to them that it isn't their responsibility to protect you. Make sure that they know how to call someone for help, where to hide during a violent incident, and practice your plan of departure with them.

Rape Safety Plan

- Go to a safe place.

- If you want to report the crime, notify the police immediately. Reporting the crime can help you regain a sense of personal power and control.

- Call a friend, a family member, or someone else you trust who can be with you and give you support.

- Preserve all physical evidence of the assault. Do not shower, bathe, douche, eat, drink, wash your hands, or brush your teeth until after you have had a medical examination. Save all of the clothing you were wearing at the time of the assault. Place each item of clothing in a separate paper bag. Do not use plastic bags. Do not clean or disturb anything in the area where the assault occurred.

- Get medical care as soon as possible. Go to a hospital emergency department or a specialized forensic clinic that provides treatment for sexual assault victims. Even if you think that you do not have any physical injuries, you should still have a medical examination and discuss with a health care provider the risk of exposure to sexually transmitted infections and the possibility of pregnancy resulting from the sexual assault. Having a medical exam is also a way for you to preserve physical evidence of a sexual assault.

- If you suspect that you may have been given a "rape drug," ask the hospital or clinic where you receive medical care to take a urine sample. Drugs, such as Rohypnol and GHB, are more likely to be detected in urine than in blood.

- Write down as much as you can remember about the circumstances of the assault, including a description of the assailant.

- Get information whenever you have questions or concerns. After a sexual assault, you have a lot of choices and decisions to make - e.g., about getting medical care, making a police report, and telling other people. You may have concerns about the impact of the assault and the reactions of friends and family members. You can get information by calling a rape crisis center, a hotline, or other victim assistance agencies.

- Talk with a counselor who is trained to assist rape victims. Counseling can help you learn how to cope with the emotional and physical impacts of the assault. You can find a counselor by contacting a local rape crisis center, a hotline, a counseling service, other victim assistance agencies, or RAINN. RAINN is a national victim assistance organization, at 1-800-656-HOPE. RAINN will connect you to a rape crisis center in your area.

Making A Police Report

- If you want to make a police report, contact the police as soon as possible. Call 9-1-1. The sooner you make a report, the more likely it is that the police will be able to collect important evidence and apprehend the assailant. A prompt report can also strengthen a case for prosecution. However, even if some time has passed since you were sexually assaulted, it is never too late to make a police report or to seek help from other victim assistance agencies.

- In many communities, police officers have had special training in assisting sexual assault victims. If you want to know about the police in your area, contact a counselor or an advocate at a local rape crisis center. Rape counselors and advocates are likely to know how the police in their community usually respond to sexual assault reports. Advocates can also accompany you when you make a police report.

Resources

Dial 9-1-1 if you need immediate emergency help.

Boys Town
1-800-448-3000

For kids, teens and young adults who are depressed or faced with an overwhelming challenge.

National Child Abuse Hotline
1-800-422-4453

National Domestic Violence Hotline
1-800-799-SAFE (7233)
1-800-787-3224 (TTY)

National Eating Disorder Association
1-800-931-2237

National Human Trafficking Resource Center
1-888-373-7888

National Runaway Safeline
1-800-RUNAWAY

National Sexual Assault Hotline
1-800-656-HOPE (4673)

National Suicide Prevention
Lifeline 1-800-273-TALK
(8255)
1-888-628-9454 (Spanish)
1-800-799-4889 (TTY)

National Youth Crisis
Hotline 1-800-448-4663

A21
http://www.A21.org

Human Trafficking organization.

End Sexual Exploitation
http://endsexualexploitation.org/resources/

National Center for Missing and Exploited
Children
http://www.missingkids.com/home

National Center on Sexual
Exploitation
http://endsexualexploitation.org/

National Human Trafficking Resource Center
[NHTRC] http://traffickingresourcecenter.org

Rape, Abuse and Incest National Network [RAINN]
https://www.rainn.org/

National Runaway Safeline
http://www.1800runaway.org

Rock Paper Scissors Foundation

Non-profit organization for those who have experienced any form of abuse to include human trafficking. RPS also provides abuse awareness nationally.

http://rockpaperscissorsfoundation.org

S.A.F.E
http://selfinjury.com

1-800-DONTCUT

Substance Abuse and Mental Health Administration
http://www.samhsa.gov/find-help/national-helpline

Author Bio
Kristal Clark
Rock Paper Scissors, Founder

Kristal Clark is the CEO and Founder of the non-profit organization, Rock Paper Scissors Foundation. Kristal's organization specializes in supporting those who have been physically, mentally, sexually, and emotionally abused as well as those who have been human trafficked. Her unstoppable passion to restore people from brokenness to wholeness has pushed her to challenge others with this theme, "We can't do anything about the past, but we sure can do something about the future." Kristal holds a degree in Early Childhood Education and is thoroughly trained in human trafficking trauma care, sexual abuse, and child abuse. Not only has she shed light on this dark practice of exploitation within communities through education and awareness, but she has also joined a team of leaders engaging in campaigns that provide hope and help for those suffering in silence caused by abuse. Kristal also serves as a facilitator and leader for Celebrate Recovery. As a national speaker and certified Life Coach, Kristal has been on radio broadcasts and TV stations. She approaches life with vision, sophistication, and confidence that inspires everyone she meets.

Author Bio
Carla Yarborough
Rock Paper Scissors, President

Carla Yarborough joined the Rock Paper Scissors movement since its inception. She has a Bachelor of Science degree in Psychology with a minor in Social Science and a Master of Arts degree in Human Services with an emphasis in Community Development. With over 20 years of experience in the human services field, Carla has served a variety of populations such as the homeless, incarcerated individuals, impoverished single parents, troubled teens, domestic violence and sexually abused survivors. Carla's passion for injustices within the community supersedes her professional résumé. Her strong desire to give back can be seen in the work that she has done as a therapeutic foster parent. If left wounded, Carla believes that unhealed children become unhealed adults, which is why she is passionate about youth advocacy. She has often stated, "You can't build a thriving community until you heal its people first." It is from this framework that she has emerged as a community leader.

Notes

92475419R00065

Made in the USA
Columbia, SC
29 March 2018